What's in a Name?

by Sharon Franklin

Editorial Offices: Glenview, Illinois • Parsippany, New Jersey • New York, New York
Sales Offices: Needham, Massachusetts • Duluth, Georgia • Glenview, Illinois
Coppell, Texas • Ontario, California • Mesa, Arizona

Photographs

Every effort has been made to secure permission and provide appropriate credit for photographic material. The publisher deeply regrets any omission and pledges to correct errors called to its attention in subsequent editions.

Unless otherwise acknowledged, all photographs are the property of Scott Foresman, a division of Pearson Education.

Photo locators denoted as follows: Top (T), Center (C), Bottom (B), Left (L), Right (R), Background (Bkgd).

Opener: (C) ©Comstock Inc., (C) ©Royalty-Free/Corbis; 1 ©Comstock Inc.; 3 ©DK Images; 4 ©Thinkstock; 5 (C) MedioImages, (BL) Getty Images; 6 ©James Neilsen/AFP/Getty Images; 7 (C) Creatas, (BR) ©MedioImages/SuperStock; 8 ©Royalty-Free/Corbis; 9 (T) image100, (C) Getty Images, (B) ©Stockbyte; 10 ©Clark James Mishler/IPN; 11 (T) ©Carol Havens/Corbis, (CR) Bridgeman Art Library; 12 Ralph Talmont/©Aurora Photos; 13 Image Source; 14 (CL) AP/Wide World Photos, (BR) ©Pace Gregory/Corbis; 15 Getty Images; 17 (T) John Foxx, (C) ©Royalty-Free/Corbis, (C) ©Image Source Limited, (B) ©Royalty-Free/Corbis; 18 Brand X Pictures; 19 ©Comstock Inc.

ISBN: 0-328-13386-8

7 8 9 10 V0G1 14 13 12 11 10 09 08

Names are important. Without names, life would be very confusing. We identify ourselves with names. We name pets, towns, rivers, spaceships, and even stars. Plants and animals even have two names—a common name and a scientific name.

In this book you'll learn about names in different cultures. After reading this book, you may want to find out more about the history of your own first and last names.

This plant's common name is Zebra plant. Its scientific name is Calathea zebrina.

Hispanic Naming Traditions

In Hispanic cultures, people have more than one surname, or last name. Many surnames are combinations of both parents' surnames. A boy named Juan López Estaban has both his father's surname (López) and his mother's (Estaban).

When a woman marries, she may keep her own surname or add her husband's surname to the end of her own. If she adds his surname, she may link it with a *y*, a hyphen, or *de, del,* or *de la* (María Estaban y López).

What would your surname be in the Hispanic tradition?

Hispanic children have several first names too. José is often one of the given names, or first names, for boys and María is one of the given names for girls.

Many Hispanic families name their children after Catholic saints. Each saint has his or her own feast day. Saint Anthony of Padua's feast day, June 13, is called *El día de San Antonio de Padua*. If a baby boy is born on June 13, the baby's given name may be Antonio.

Many Hispanic children are named after the Catholic saint whose feast day is the same as their birth date.

Asian Naming Traditions

Traditionally, Chinese, Japanese, Vietnamese, and Korean names begin with the family name, or surname. Have you ever heard of the Chinese basketball player Yao Ming? Yao is his family name. Ming is his given name.

Some Asian given names are based on a theme. For example, in an Indonesian family, three children may be named Intan, which means "diamond," Perak, which means "silver," and Emas, which means "gold."

You might call this basketball player Yao, but that is really his family name. You should call him Ming.

You may have a middle name that is not used when people speak to you. However, in some Asian countries, more than one word forms a person's given name. For example, Mei Qing Hua means "beautiful blue flower." The entire name must be spoken. To shorten it would change its meaning.

Mei Qing Hua is as pretty as the beautiful blue flower that her mother named her after.

Middle Eastern Naming Traditions

In Jewish families, children may be given both an English name and a Hebrew name. The English name is used every day, while the Hebrew name is used on special occasions.

Another Jewish **custom** is to name children to honor a relative. Boys are usually given their names on the eighth day after their birth. Many parents now hold similar naming ceremonies for their daughters.

In Jewish families, a child's name is very important to his or her future. A baby's name is given eight days after he or she is born.

African Naming Traditions

The Yoruba people of Africa, who live in southwestern Nigeria, also name a child on the eighth day after he or she is born. A Yoruba naming ceremony uses many symbols. The symbols shown on this page are used in the naming ceremony for a baby. The ceremony ends with a feast and party.

money—*The baby is shown money. If he or she reaches for it, he or she will have wealth.*

meat—*The baby is given a small bite of food to remind him or her of all that nature provides.*

water—*Water patted on the baby's face reminds him or her of nature's cleansing qualities.*

oil—*Oil dabbed on the baby's face is to give him or her peace and calm during hard times.*

salt and sugar—*A taste of each is given to improve the baby's sense of taste and bring happiness.*

cola nut—*A taste of cola nut represents a long life.*

ginger—*A taste of ginger symbolizes good health.*

Haida Naming Traditions

The Queen Charlotte Islands are off the west coast of Canada. The northernmost island, Graham, is home to the Haida people.

Haida objects, including totem poles and button blankets, are decorated with crests. To the Haida people, a crest is like a name. Wherever you go, your crest tells people where you are from and who your relatives are.

A potlatch is a formal ceremony that includes feasting, speeches, singing, dancing, and gift-giving. A special naming potlatch honors the one who is named, and they are given a unique button blanket decorated with the family crest.

The Haida people decorate their totem poles and button blankets with crests that represent a family's history.

The buttons on button blankets were once made from abalone shells. Now mother-of-pearl is used. The Haida believe that the more buttons there are on a blanket, the more power the person who owns the blanket has. One button blanket had more than 1,700 buttons!

Maori Naming Traditions

Long ago, New Zealand's Maori people performed an ancient ceremony to name a child. People gathered to greet the child and welcome him or her into the world. They brought food as gifts, and there was singing and feasting.

The ceremony took place in a river or stream. People faced east. A priest stood in the water and held the child up to the sky as he said the child's name. Another priest would release a bird and allow it to fly away.

The Maori culture and language is passed on from parents to children.

Changing Names

People change their names for many reasons. When they marry, many American women drop their family names and take their husbands' family names. Other times, the couple may create a last name that combines both of their names. John Stephens and Mary Abbot become John and Mary Stephens Abbot. Sometimes a hyphen is added between the two last names.

When Americans marry, they can choose to keep their own surnames or make up a new one.

Famous people do not become famous **overnight.** It can take years to become well-known to the **public,** so some entertainers change their names to one that people can remember easily.

Some **popular** musicians change their names to just one word. We know Paul David Hewson as Bono. Madonna Louise Veronica Ciccone put a simple **twist** on her long name by shortening it to Madonna.

Some famous people change or shorten their real names, including Bono and Madonna.

Nicknames

Nicknames are a popular way to change your name. Many nicknames are short versions of a person's name. Michael may be known as Mike, or Jennifer may like to be called Jenny.

Even pets can have nicknames! Sometimes people show their pets in competitions. The pet may have a long name used just for those events. At home, the pet may be called by a nickname. A pet's name may also be shortened. Pouncer could become Pounce, or Mittens could become Mitt.

Does your pet have a nickname? Did you get to pick it out?

Exact Meaning

Many people can learn something about their family histories by studying their surnames.

Some surnames help identify an ancestor's name. The Swedish name Johnson means "son of John." The prefix, or beginning, of some Irish surnames also gives clues about family relationships. The "O" in O'Callahan means "grandson of." The "Mac" in MacDonald means "son of."

A name can give other information. For example, the surnames Strong and Small give clues to what the people with these names were like. West and Field relate to location and nature. Other surnames, such as Miller, Farmer, and Weaver, describe people's jobs.

Surnames and given names have exact meanings in many different cultures.

Given Names for Girls

Deborah (Hebrew) – bee

Afina (Rumanian) – blueberry

Margaret (Latin) – pearl

Bethany (Hebrew) – house

Given Names for Boys

Aran (Thai) – the forest

Oliver (French) – olive tree

Clifford (English) – from a steep cliff

Anwar (African) – the brightest

Surnames

Baker – job

Woods – nature

Fast – quality

Williamson – son of William

Namesakes

Names are chosen carefully and often have special meaning. Many children are named after someone their parents **admire.** Your middle name may be your grandmother's given name. You may be named after a friend or a famous person such as a scientist, author, or president.

Were you named after someone else in your family?

A Final Word on Names

Our names are important to us and to others. It is important to remember to be respectful when meeting someone, especially if the name or culture of the person is new to you.

When you are introduced, listen carefully. Try to pronounce the name and ask if you are saying it correctly. If you are curious, you may ask how the person got his or her name. You may **mention** what you know about your own name as well.

Glossary

admire *v.* to look at with wonder, pleasure, and approval.

custom *n.* old or popular way of doing things.

famous *adj.* very well known; noted.

mention *v.* to tell or speak about something.

overnight *adv.* during the night.

popular *adj.* liked by most people.

public *adj.* of or for everyone; belonging to the people.

twist *n.* an unexpected variation.